RENFREWSHIRE'S LAST DAYS OF :

by
W.A.C. Smith

The Paisley & Renfrew Railway was Renfrewshire's earliest passenger carrying line, but by the 1950s the service had dwindled to half a dozen trains which ran at times suitable only to shift workers. However, on 14 September 1959 the semi-derelict Renfrew (Wharf) Station – the wharf itself had been demolished by a wartime bomb – played host to an excursion for the Scottish Industries Exhibition at Kelvin Hall, headed by a pair of preserved locomotives in their colourful liveries. Caledonian Railway 4-2-2, no. 123, dated from 1886 while the Jones Goods 4-6-0, no. 103, had been built in 1894 for the Highland Railway. Both are now housed in the Glasgow Museum of Transport.

Text and photographs © W.A.C. Smith, 2002.
First published in the United Kingdom, 2002,
by Stenlake Publishing.
Telephone / Fax: 01290 551122

ISBN 1 84033 191 7

A rebuilt Patriot 4-6-0, no. 45527, 'Southport', approaches Hillington (West) on the four track Paisley Joint line with the 6.55 a.m. mail and parcels train from Carlisle to Glasgow Parcels Station, routed via Kilmarnock and Dalry, on 25 June 1964. Upon electrification the Paisley line was reduced to double track.

Opposite: A memory of the time when Elderslie not only had a passenger station (boasting a pair of island platforms) and a busy freight yard, but was also junction for the Greenock (Princes Pier) line, and associated Lochwinnoch loop, and gave access to the Paisley (Canal) line which formed a useful diversionary route for Glasgow. On 27 July 1955 Jubilee 4-6-0 no. 45707, 'Valiant', passes at speed with 'The Irishman', having left Glasgow (St Enoch) at 8.45 p.m. with the service to Stranraer Harbour where it would connect with the overnight sailing to Larne.

INTRODUCTION

Although Renfrewshire had few pioneering wagonways to form the basis of a transport system, a railway (of 4 foot 6 inch gauge) from Paisley to Renfrew was authorised as early as 1835 and opened two years later. In 1837 both the Glasgow, Paisley, Kilmarnock & Ayr Railway and the Glasgow, Paisley & Greenock Railway received the Royal Assent, and these companies arranged that the section between Glasgow and Paisley should be made as a joint railway. This opened in 1840 together with the line to Ayr. The GPK&A amalgamated with the Glasgow, Dumfries & Carlisle Railway in 1850 to form the Glasgow & South Western Railway, while the following year the Glasgow, Paisley & Greenock Railway, which had opened in 1841, was acquired by the Caledonian Railway. The Greenock Works became the locomotive works for the Caledonian Railway, but were replaced in 1856 by the St Rollox establishment in Springburn, Glasgow.

The Greenock company had pioneered combined rail and steamboat services and these were dramatically expanded when the Caledonian, at very considerable expense, extended the railway to Gourock in 1889, this section including the longest tunnel in Scotland. The Caledonian (the 'Caley') had worked the Wemyss Bay Railway, opened from Port Glasgow in 1865, and with acquisition of this concern in 1893 the track was partly doubled and the station and pier at Wemyss Bay rebuilt in lavish fashion to serve Caledonian Steam Packet Co. sailings to Bute and Cumbrae. In the early years there had been several proposals to extend the railway from Wemyss Bay to Largs, but nothing came of those.

Meanwhile, the Glasgow & South Western (the 'Sou'West') had not been idle and reached Greenock in 1869 by means of the steeply graded Greenock & Ayrshire Railway which had originated in 1864 as the Bridge of Weir Railway. A new terminal at Greenock Princes Pier was brought into use in 1894 for G&SW steamer services and, with the North British Railway having opened its Craigendoran terminal on the North bank in 1883, fierce competition ensued between all three companies for Clyde Coast traffic.

At a more local level the Renfrew line was connected to the Paisley Joint line in 1866, the Busby Railway (later acquired by the Caledonian and extended to East Kilbride) was opened, and the Glasgow, Barrhead & Kilmarnock Joint Railway was completed in 1873. Also, the Paisley Canal Line, constructed partly on the course of the never completed Glasgow, Paisley & Ardrossan Canal, opened in 1885. The Potterhill branch from Paisley was opened in 1886, being extended to Barrhead in 1902, and the short-lived Glasgow & Renfrew District Railway, worked alternatively by the Caledonian and G&SW, followed in 1903. The last major constructions were the North Johnstone line, opened by the G&SW in 1905 to relieve pressure on the original line along the east side of the Castle Semple loch, and the Caledonian Lanarkshire & Ayrshire route to Ardrossan which was completed, running through Whitecraigs and Uplawmoor, in 1903.

Both railway companies in Renfrewshire came under LMS (Northern Division) control in 1923 and upon nationalisation in 1948 formed part of the Scottish Region of British Railways. Fifty years later this reverted to private ownership under the somewhat odd title of Scotrail Railways Limited. Notwithstanding electrification to Neilston (1962), Gourock and Wemyss Bay (1967), and Ayr and Largs (1986), Renfrewshire has shared in the countrywide decline in rail services. The closures of the Princes Pier line, Lochwinnoch loop, and Renfrew branch were notable examples, although closures had in fact commenced many years before with the withdrawal of the G&SW service between Paisley and Barrhead in 1913 (a competing Caledonian line was never completed), and the Glasgow & Renfrew District Railway from Cardonald did not reopen for passengers after the 1926 General Strike. More recently, closure of the Canal Line in 1983, followed by its costly reopening seven years later, but not unfortunately as a through route, was an astonishing example of management incompetence from Strathclyde Passenger Transport, as is the continuing lack of a rail connection to Glasgow Airport.

In conclusion, it may be noted that Renfrewshire had the dubious distinction of hosting the last Scottish Region steam hauled passenger workings. These ended on 28 April, 1967.

BR standard 2-6-4T no. 80008 leaving Paisley (Gilmour Street) with a 'Cunarder' liner special from Greenock (Princes Pier) to Glasgow (Central) on 3 November 1955. On the right is 2-6-4T no. 42259 of LMS design with the 12.05 p.m. service from Gourock. The Joint line had been quadrupled in the early 1880s, at which time the station at Paisley was reconstructed with four platforms. It received the distinguishing suffix of Gilmour Street upon the opening of St James Station on the Gourock line in 1883.

Class 6P 4-6-2 no. 72009, 'Clan Stewart', pauses at Paisley (Gilmour Street) with the 11.44 a.m. from Stranraer (Town) to Glasgow (St Enoch) on 29 September 1952. The Clans, of British Railways construction and forming part of a series of standard designs, met with a mixed reception from footplate crews when introduced in 1952. No. 72009 certainly appears to be leaking an excessive amount of steam for a locomotive barely six months old.

A very typical Renfrewshire railway scene of forty or more years ago as 2-6-4T no. 42202 leaves Milliken Park with the 10.10 a.m. train from Ayr to Glasgow (St Enoch) on 20 June 1959. It is passing the former G&SW signal box, semaphore signals, and a permanent way ganger's bothy.

Standard Five no. 73005 passing the former Howwood Station (opened by the G&SW in 1876 and closed by BR in 1955) with the 6.10 p.m. Campbeltown steamer connection from Fairlie Pier to Glasgow (St Enoch) on 30 July 1963. Howwood Station was reopened in 2000.

As Black Five no. 45489 approaches Howwood with the 6.25 p.m. from Glasgow (St Enoch) to Kilmarnock via Dalry on 30 July 1963, it passes the cottages of permanent way (i.e. the track) staff. The immaculate condition of their permanent way is noteworthy.

Black Five no. 44881 passing Lochside Station on 25 June 1955 – its day of closure – with a down freight. With the closure of the Lochwinnoch loop in 1966 Lochside Station was reopened and renamed Lochwinnoch.

Standard 2-6-4T no. 80112 arrives at a snow covered Lochwinnoch Station on 27 November 1965 with the 1315 from Glasgow (St Enoch) to Kilmarnock via Dalry. The twenty-four hour clock had been brought into use with that year's summer timetable.

The Bridge of Weir Railway was opened from Johnstone in 1864 and upon its merging with the Greenock & Ayrshire Railway five years later a new connection for Glasgow traffic was provided at Elderslie. The Cart Junction to Johnstone Curve was retained (although without a regular passenger service after 1900) and on 4 July 1959 was traversed by class 4MT 2-6-0 no. 76095 with a 9.38 a.m. holiday special from Greenock (Princes Pier) to Girvan.

Standard 2-6-4T no. 80127 at Bridge of Weir with the 2.20 p.m. from Greenock (Princes Pier) to Glasgow (St Enoch) on 26 May 1956. Opened in 1869, this through station replaced the original terminal of the single track Bridge of Weir Railway which was situated to the right and at a slightly lower level. The Kilmacolm branch, as it became with the closure of Greenock (Princes Pier), was abandoned in 1983.

In steam days the annual Orange Walks put much traffic on the railways. On 6 July 1963 there were eleven specials to Greenock, six using the town's Lynedoch Station with the others arriving at Central Station. Five of the trains to Lynedoch originated at Glasgow (St Enoch) and, with each loading to ten coaches, these were double headed. The 10.10 a.m. special with class 4MT 2-6-0 no. 76091 piloting 2-6-4T no. 80030 is pictured passing Kilmacolm on the 1 in 101 climb to Upper Port Glasgow. From there the line fell at a gradient of 1 in 98/70 to Greenock (Lynedoch) Station and then went through a pair of tunnels to the terminus at Greenock (Princes Pier).

Class 3F 0-6-0 no. 57566 gathers speed from Upper Port Glasgow on the downhill dash to Greenock with the 3.05 p.m. from Glasgow (St Enoch) to Greenock (Princes Pier) on 7 August 1954. Built by the Caledonian Railway in 1899 this locomotive has been preserved and can be found on the Strathspey Railway at Aviemore.

From Upper Port Glasgow signal box and siding there was a panoramic view across the Firth of Clyde to the mountains of Argyll. Pictured on 7 August 1954, 2-6-4T no. 42688 approaches with the 3.30 p.m. from Greenock (Princes Pier) to Glasgow (St Enoch). It then turned inland, topped the 1 in 98 gradient after a further half mile, and swept down across moorland to Kilmacolm.

Greenock (Lynedoch) Station was situated in the upper part of the town and is pictured on 4 May 1957 with former Caledonian Railway 4-4-0 no. 54506 leaving with the 5.07 p.m. from Glasgow (St Enoch) and about to enter the tunnels down to the terminus at Greenock (Princes Pier).

Greenock (Lynedoch) Station pictured from the east on 23 August 1958. Standard 2-6-4T no. 80002 was calling with the 3.30 p.m. from Greenock (Princes Pier) to Glasgow (St Enoch). This locomotive is preserved on the Keighley & Worth Valley Railway. Note the new mineral wagons stored in the goods siding.

Princes Pier locomotive shed occupied an extremely awkward site between the tunnel mouth and the terminus and there were frequent complaints from nearby householders about the smoke nuisance, hence the oddly shaped roof vents. Former Caledonian Railway 4-4-0s monopolised the service between the late 1930s and the early 1950s and on 1 August 1953 one of these sturdy machines, no. 54453, was pictured being coaled while 2-6-4T no. 42691, a recent transfer from Polmadie shed, was taking water. The depot was closed in 1959 following the cutting back of the passenger service to Kilmacolm, although servicing facilities were retained for several more years.

In the glorious summer of 1955 the annual West of Scotland Orange Walk was held at Greenock's Battery Park on 9 July with twelve specials arriving at Greenock (Lynedoch) and five at Greenock (Central). The Lynedoch trains returned from Greenock (Princes Pier) and the first departure was seventeen minutes late at 5.12 p.m. with standard 2-6-4T no. 80023 assisting the former LNER class V1 2-6-2T, no. 67661, as far as Bridge of Weir on the nine coach train bound for Bellgrove on the Glasgow (Queen Street) low level line.

Despite the plethora of Caledonian bogies at Princes Pier motive power depot in the early 1950s, an occasional motive power shortage would result in the activation of locomotives euphemistically described as 'stored serviceable' (i.e. they were supposedly available for service if required). At Princes Pier these were generally compound 4-4-0s built in the early days of the LMS in the 1920s for main line work, but replaced by larger locomotives in the 1930s. Thus, on 18 September 1951, the resurrected no. 41148 headed the 5.25 p.m. for Glasgow. It was scrapped some eighteen months later.

On a bright April afternoon in 1952 class 3P ex-Caledonian 4-4-0 no. 54508 made an attractive picture as it awaited departure from Greenock (Princes Pier) with the 3.30 p.m. train for Glasgow (St Enoch). Carried on the locomotive's front bufferbeam is the Caledonian type route indicator which confirmed the train's destination to signalmen on the route.

In September 1952 there was a three day visit to the Clyde by seventy warships, among them the battleships HMS *Vanguard* and USS *Wisconsin* and six aircraft carriers, prior to a large scale NATO exercise codenamed 'Operation Mainbrace'. With 10,000 seamen being given shore leave each afternoon, five special trains were run from Greenock (Princes Pier) to Paisley and Glasgow, returning in the late evening, together with six from Gourock. There were also excursions from Glasgow (St Enoch) for cruises around the fleet. This was the animated scene at Greenock (Princes Pier) on the afternoon of 12 September, with the 2.15 p.m. naval leave special loading at platform four while 2-6-4T no. 42195 (centre) waits at platform three with the 2.30 p.m. special. Caledonian 4-4-0 no. 54457, borrowed from Ladyburn shed to act as station pilot, is at platform two.

Class 4F 0-6-0 no. 44196 shunts empty coaching stock at Greenock (Princes Pier) on 12 August 1955 before working the 7.15 p.m. goods service to Glasgow (High Street). 2-6-4T no. 42122 was on a 'Cunarder', leaving for Glasgow (Central) at 6.39 p.m. with passengers off the liner *Parthia*.

Standard class 4MT 2-6-0 no. 76090 pictured on arrival at platform two of Greenock (Princes Pier) with the 3.05 p.m. from Glasgow (St Enoch) on 3 August 1957. This Saturdays only service was worked by a Corkerhill engine which returned with Irish cattle from the Albert Harbour lairage which was alongside Princes Pier. The passenger service from Princes Pier ended on 31 January 1959, being cut back to Kilmacolm. The last up train at 8.48 p.m., hauled by 2-6-4T no. 42190, departed to a fusilade of a hundred or more detonaters! The last arrival (at ten minutes to midnight) was pulled by 2-6-4T no. 42238. 'Cunarder' and 'Empress Voyager' liner specials continued until 1965. The station and imposing Italianate buildings on the pier were demolished in 1967 for construction of the Clydeport container terminal.

Paisley (West) Station on the Canal line was opened in 1897 and closed in 1966. On 30 April 1965 standard 2-6-4T no. 80047, having worked the 5.13 p.m. local train from Glasgow (St Enoch), runs round the empty stock on the surviving portion of the Barrhead branch (which served a chocolate warehouse at Potterhill) and is drawing into the up platform to form the 5.46 p.m. back to Glasgow.

BR Standard class 4 4-6-0s were never allocated to the Scottish Region, but in the last years of steam several were overhauled at Cowlairs and St Rollox works and were to be seen on test runs (or 'runnning-in turns') afterwards. On 27 August 1965 double chimney no. 75026, a former Western Region locomotive which by then was with the London Midland Region and shedded at Liverpool (Bank Hall), was used for the 1713 train from Glasgow (St Enoch) to Paisley (West) and is pictured at Hawkhead on the 1746 return working.

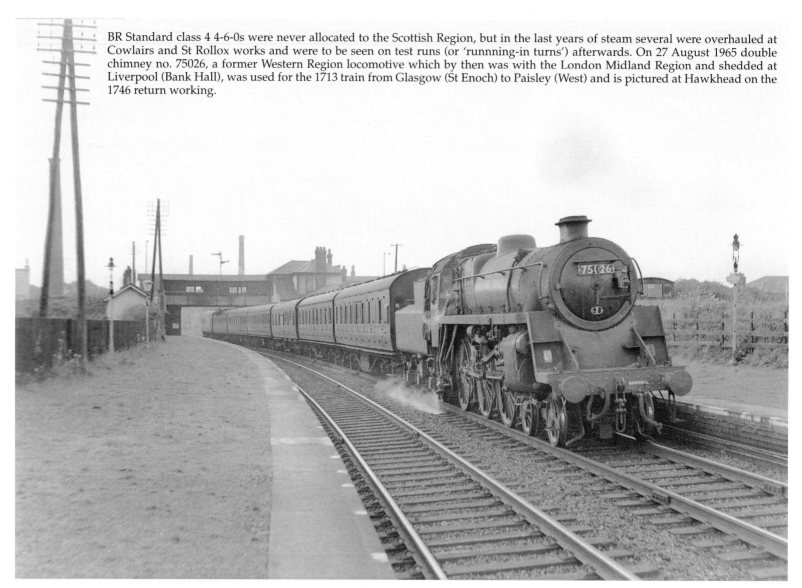

'Starlight Specials' were introduced in April 1953, providing cheap overnight travel between Glasgow (St Enoch) and London (St Pancras) at a fare of seventy shillings for an eight or fifteen day stay. The outward journey was made on a Friday night and over the following ten years the trains proved so popular that a dozen or more were necessary on occasions. On 14 July – Fair Friday – 1961 there were seven departures and this was the first of these, the 5.00 p.m., passing Barrhead with Black Five no. 44900 piloting rebuilt Scot no. 46130, 'The West Yorkshire Regiment', on twelve coaches. Increasing car ownership and cheap overseas holidays brought a decline in patronage and the 'Starlights' were discontinued after the summer of 1962.

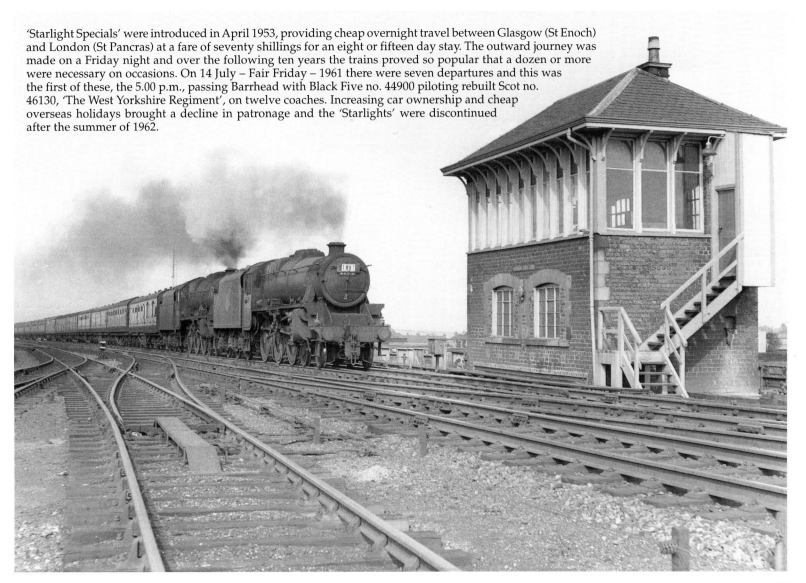

Jubilee 4-6-0 no. 45727, 'Inflexible', and A3 4-6-2 no. 60086, 'Gainsborough', tackle the 1 in 69 gradient of Neilston bank with the 6.38 p.m. car sleeper from Glasgow (St Enoch) to London (Marylebone) on 23 July 1962. The LNER Pacifics carried the names of race horses, Gainsborough being the winner of the Derby, the two thousand guineas and the St Leger.

Class 3MT 2-6-2T no. 40176 calling at Whitecraigs on the Lanarkshire & Ayrshire line with the 12.11 p.m. from Glasgow (Central) to Neilston (High) on 11 November 1955. Whitecraigs Station is adjacent to Rouken Glen Park and before the First World War it had the unusual distinction of having a summer Sunday service of ten trains in the days when little in the way of public transport disturbed the tranquility of the Scottish Sabbath. The LMS 2-6-2Ts were a not particularly successful design dating from 1935 and were more often to be found on the Glasgow (Central) low level system.

In preparation for inauguration of the Glasgow South electrification scheme of 1962 the passenger service between Neilston and Uplawmoor ended on 31 March that year. The last train, the 1.13 p.m. from Glasgow (Central), is pictured upon its punctual arrival at Uplawmoor at 1.55 p.m., hauled by 2-6-4T no. 42246. This section of the erstwhile Lanarkshire & Ayrshire line, which although it had not been a through route to Ardrossan since 1939 still provided a useful link with the Glasgow, Barrhead & Kilmarnock route at Lugton, was abandoned less than three years later. The name Uplawmoor was transferred to the nearby Glasgow, Barrhead & Kilmarnock station at Caldwell until its closure in 1966.

In 1959 trains on the former Caledonian Railway branch from Glasgow to East Kilbride were transferred from Central to St Enoch and dieselised but for two peak period workings in each direction which remained steam worked until 1966. On 21 August 1964 standard 2-6-4T no. 80108 was pictured arriving at Thornliebank, one of the three Renfrewshire stations on the branch, with the 8.18 a.m. from East Kilbride.

The steam trains returned to East Kilbride from Glasgow (St Enoch) at 5.08 p.m. and 5.33 p.m. Monday to Friday, the coaches being stabled at East Kilbride overnight. On 19 June 1964 standard 2-6-4T no. 80109 was skirting Williamwoood golf course as it approached Clarkston with the 5.33 p.m. train.

On 27 November 1965 there had been an early snowfall as standard tank no. 80122 left Paisley (Gilmour Street) with the 1110 from Glasgow (Central) to Gourock, replacing a diesel multiple unit. The photograph was taken from Stoneybrae signal box, situated between the Gourock and Ayr lines, which was replaced exactly one year later by the new Paisley box.

2-6-4T no. 42197 arriving at Paisley (St James) with the 1300 from Gourock to Glasgow (Central) on 15 March 1966. The never completed Paisley & Barrhead District Railway leads off to the left immediately beyond the platform.

Had a Paisley and Barrhead District passenger service materialised in all probability it would have been worked by Caledonian 0-4-4Ts, one of which, no. 55225, is pictured here on 6 June 1960 near Linwood on the truncated line.

In the previous picture no. 55225, which had been built in 1914, was on its way to the Pressed Steel Co. works to collect one of the new Blue Trains being built for the forthcoming Glasgow Suburban Electrification from Airdrie to Helensburgh and branches. This is it on its return journey to the Hyndland depot. These well liked and reliable electric units are only now being replaced after more than forty years service.

By 1963 the Paisley & Barrhead Railway was disused beyond Chain Road sidings at Ferguslie and the station there, which was never opened for passengers, was visited on 23 March of that year by a Branch Line Society railtour composed of eight goods brake vans hauled by former Caledonian Railway 0-6-0, no. 57689. The station buildings had been demolished by then, but I had photographed those at Stanley, the next station along the line and which would have been similar, on 20 December 1955, by which time they were occupied as a private dwelling.

After calling at Bishopton and leaving closed Georgetown Station behind, standard 2-6-4T no. 80130 accelerates past Blackstone signal box on 22 March 1960 with the 11.30 a.m. from Wemyss Bay to Glasgow (Central). The freight only Linwood branch diverged here. Built by James Dunlop & Co. to serve an ironstone pit, the branch was acquired by the Caledonian Railway in the 1880s, but is now closed along with a connection to the former Clippens Oil Works.

Standard class 5 no. 73072 runs into the riverside station of Langbank with the 6.25 p.m. train from Glasgow (Central) to Wemyss Bay on 2 July 1960. With electrification Langbank has gained an improved service, but inevitably the not unattractive station buildings have been replaced by tawdry shelters.

On 25 April 1959 2-6-4T no. 42243 awaits departure from Port Glasgow with the 9.45 a.m. train from Gourock to Glasgow (Central). The station had been rebuilt by the Caledonian Railway around 1912.

The west end of Port Glasgow Station on 29 September 1962. The train is the 3.20 p.m. from Glasgow (Central) to Gourock headed by 2-6-4T no. 42691, a type of locomotive which monopolised Clyde Coast services during the BR steam era. The bay platform (now removed) was used to provide connections for local stations from limited stop boat trains.

Shipyard cranes form a backdrop as one of the ubiquitous 2-6-4Ts, no. 42266, calls at Bogston Station with the 5.43 p.m. from Glasgow to Gourock on 10 June 1965.

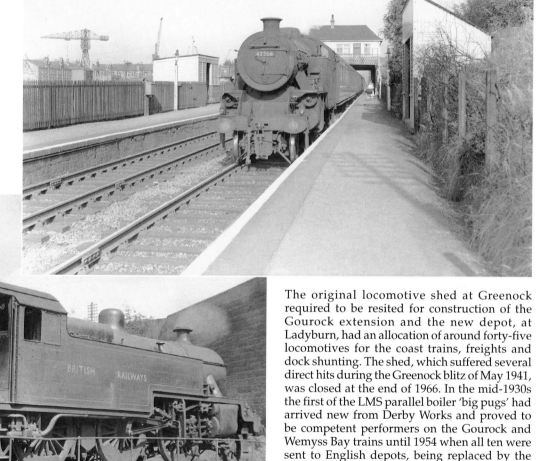

The original locomotive shed at Greenock required to be resited for construction of the Gourock extension and the new depot, at Ladyburn, had an allocation of around forty-five locomotives for the coast trains, freights and dock shunting. The shed, which suffered several direct hits during the Greenock blitz of May 1941, was closed at the end of 1966. In the mid-1930s the first of the LMS parallel boiler 'big pugs' had arrived new from Derby Works and proved to be competent performers on the Gourock and Wemyss Bay trains until 1954 when all ten were sent to English depots, being replaced by the taper boiler variant already seen in these pages. This is no. 42416 on the Ladyburn turntable on 1 August 1953.

Class 4 2-6-4T no. 42258 at Greenock (Central) with the 5.00 p.m. train from Gourock to Glasgow (Central) on 3 August 1957. The station, on the site of the original Cathcart Street terminus, lost its roof during the Greenock blitz when the town was attacked by 250 Luftwaffe bombers.

Black Five no. 45012 leaves Gourock on 10 June 1965 with the 4.35 p.m. for Glasgow. The photograph was taken from the Cardwell Bay footbridge which was removed upon electrification of the line in 1967. In the background are the goods shed and carriage sidings while on the right is the locomotive siding and Caledonian Steam Packet Co. berths. During the Second World War these berths were occupied by dozens of convoy escort vessels.

There was never a locomotive shed at Gourock, but watering facilities and a turntable were provided until the end of steam working. On 28 September 1965 standard 2-6-4T no. 80116 was being turned after working the 1557 train from Glasgow (the twenty-four hour clock had by then been introduced).

Black Five no. 45342 pictured on arrival at platform one of Gourock terminus with the 1725 from Glasgow (Central) on 3 June 1966. This London Midland Region locomotive, shedded at Carnforth, had been overhauled at Cowlairs Works which retained the former LNER practice of stencilling the shed name on the front bufferbeam. Today this platform, now renumbered as three, has been much shortened.

Although partially doubled under Caledonian auspices the ten mile Wemyss Bay branch from Port Glasgow included a single line section from Greenock Upper to Dunrod. On 26 April 1960 the signalman at the latter place was handing the tablet authorising entry to the single track to the fireman of 2-6-4T no. 42243 which was working the 5.30 p.m. train from Wemyss Bay to Glasgow. Upon electrification the branch reverted to single track with Dunrod becoming a passing place.

2-6-4T no. 42144 emerging from Inverkip tunnel with the 3.30 p.m. from Wemyss Bay to Glasgow on 26 April 1960. This section had been doubled in 1903 and the bore on the left was made at that time. It was abandoned upon electrification in 1967.

Ex-LMS 'Crab' 2-6-0 no. 42740 at Wemyss Bay on 26 April 1960 with the 2.15 p.m. train for Glasgow (Central) connecting with the car ferry 'Cowal' from Rothesay. The station, a Grade A listed structure which has recently been refurbished, replaced the original terminus in 1903 and has two sinuously curved platforms, glazed canopies, clock tower, semicircular concourse and covered ramp leading to the pier. The last steam train from Wemyss Bay ran on 26 February 1966, hauled by Black Five no. 44878.